The Powerful Voice of
Jennifer Diskin

AUTHOR STAR #2121

ISBN-13: 978-1-940-927-27-5

MAJOR STAR PUBLISHING

Imprint of Quincentennial Publishing Company

www.majorstar.us

A LIGHT OMNI MEDIA PRODUCTION

Published in the United States of America

Major Star
Publishing

Estate Approval and Executive Director: Edmund Diskin

Executive Producer & Publisher: John Errigo, Ph.D.

Cover design and Jacket by: John Errigo, PhD.

Jacket photos & concept by: Megan Diskin Monahan, Ph.D.

Release Date: 29 JAN 2020 | Second Pressing: Feb 1, 2020

THE
QUIET LILAC
COLLECTION
The Powerful Voice of
Jennifer Diskin

Publisher's Notes -Hamilton, New Jersey:

I was contacted by Jennifer Diskin's family in the fall of 2016 to publish Jennifer's poetry. Jennifer and I met in the fall of 2000 and we were introduced by her sister Megan. From 2000 to 2005 (until I moved to Philly), Jennifer and I were always together. We went out weekly to the clubs, to makeshift yoga "studios" (we paid $5.00 to do yoga in basements of churches and at West Scranton Intermediate School), and we spent an inordinate amount of time at Borders, B&N, and local diners. I fell in love with Jennifer's poetry and how she nostalgically could craft and powerfully emote a poem that nobody else would dare. The one major regret I had at Jennifer's funeral and beyond, was that she deserved to have the "big stage" and professional accolades that any other big talent would receive. Jennifer was talented but my dear friend.

When contemplating the best course of action for publication, I felt it was best for a tribute book –a major collection of Jennifer's work to date. This book includes 3 parts; a book of new poems, Book I: ("The Hard Shove of Snow"), and Book II: Published selections from "Wear White and Grieve," and Book III: "Transplanted poems," (some unreleased). Thank you to Dawn Leas, M.F.A., and Richard Aston who edited a collection of Jennifer's poems entitled "The Hard Shove of Snow."

I am grateful to the Diskin family: Ed, Tara, and Brian Diskin. Special thanks to Megan, who was very helpful (like a GPS guide) during this project. Lastly, I will not receive any royalties from this book. The family intends to donate all book royalties to charitable causes. It is my hope that this book will become a classic and will be admired by every serious poet. Best of love to my beloved friend Jennifer whom I miss dearly. Best wishes to a smashing success for her new book (a tribute to her talent).

John Errigo, Ph.D. | Publisher | **Major Star Publishing** | Jan 29, 2020

Dedication

To the Memory of Anita Diskin, loving wife and mother and to her daughter Jennifer.

Family's Special Thanks

Dawn and John

Table of Contents Book I, II & III
The Quiet Lilac Collection
The Powerful Voice of Jennifer Diskin

Book I |The Hard Shove of Snow| Page

"This quick fall allows winter
to blow in
and leave January
lounging along evergreens."

The Powerful Voice of
Jennifer Diskin

"Leaves change, though.
Love, she remembers
is the space between seasons
when his fingers
brush her hands
right before sleep.
She doesn't want to leave
and hesitates as she walks out
the kitchen door."

"The Italian festival has the tents up.
The summer's over
except for cannoils and ziti and meatballs
The best I can do
is surrender
to homemade sauces and cheesecakes
all delights so sweet
you would think paradise is
right here on North Washington St. and Linden Ave.
right above the electric lights of Scranton."

"A coffee table on ancient movie starlets.
Knick knack guardian angels
eavesdrop for gossip.
of Joan Crawford's downfall
from *Mommie Dearest* to *Baby Jane*."

The Powerful Voice of
Jennifer Diskin

"

Saying goodbye is never easy.
Qualify the word never
and question why
I put it in a sentence."

"At 9:03,
A thousand alphabets speak
running down stairs
or flying out windows."

Serious Illness At Arby's Restaurant, Great Bend

We stopped
for a roast beef sandwich,
as if the salt in the meat
wouldn't sting
what I chew.

"I'm sick,"
I muttered
dipping the fry
into the ketchup
and taking a sip
of soda.

"Not long 'til we get home."
I add.
I finish the sandwich
before the appetite goes
under fluorescent lights
and orange plastic seats

"I know."
he says.
He puts his hand out
across the table
to hold mine
as if this were enough
to take away
what happens
after you finish eating.

At The Edge of The Everyday

The Ajax bottle
stands dutiful
by the sink
waiting for a chance
to scour away
the dirt
around the edges.

I twist my silver necklace
with a cross dangling
and wonder
how polite I must be
with jewelry
before it breaks.

Test Pattern

The lady said,
"Breathe in and breathe out."
and so I did.

All I can do now
is listen to other's commands
and just do
what they say.

I can't even write
decent poems
with line breaks
that make sense.

I take tests
for heart and lung functions.

While I wait
for a transplant,
I type away
at this computer
try to find an alphabet
someone loves.

Broken News

The thrift store obituaries
are as coveted by the noontime crowd
as a BLT
on toasted rye.
No one accounts for lost keys
or empty beds
after breath walks out the door
for good.
Our days tuck into the B section
folded, read and back together again.
One and two syllable nouns
verbs and some adjectives
thrown in for fluff.

Our practical story lines
mention church, significant relatives
and job occupations.
but don't let the news
quote the heart's putter.

When we create kindness
from our body,
the moment of unconditional love
makes paradise
for a minute or two
then stops.

Play Catch

During the Superbowl,
you want
to be selfish.

You mention a cashier
at the supermarket,
blonde and healthy.

I can't stand
to hear about
perfect checkout girls.

How do I compete
with a girl with curls
bouncing up and down?

I won't.

At Ease

Forks and knives
stand at attention
on the table.

The chairs
lined up
as soldiers
meeting the sergeant
for the first time.

Rigid backs
with no room
for the body
to move anywhere.

No time to daydream
in a kitchen
like this.

Dead Upon Arrival

The sun stabs daffodils
and opens
a white and yellow homicide.

A hibachi holds
last year's charcoals.
One huge satellite dish
gets soccer
on a good day.

An elm lined street
has one nosy neighbor:
a hospital.

Across the street,
clogged hearts
lay in antiseptic beds.

Inside the house,
he flips the channels
on the TV.

Her kisses
the one calm.

He pulls away.

Overweight

I struggle to
button my pants.
I can't wear
my shirt over jeans.

No one shouts
"You're sick."
or "You're getting fat."

A poinsettia lounges
on the kitchen table.

The laundry waits
to be folded
and put away.

Chicken soup
boils in the pot.

There are no metaphors
in a life
cruel with facts.

Drafted

The draft from
the window comes

whether or not
I insulate the window.

The cold jabbers his way
into the house.

He is a
snow salesman

and sells
the ice

without asking
how I will pay

for the large price.
He has shiny white teeth

and tells me
I can't refuse.

So I buy
and buy some more.

I know
when spring arrives

he'll come again
beg for more scratch

and I will give him
the money.

His voice
convinces.

I just can't say no
even though

I remember the word frozen.
Wanting

Blankets unfurl
like tattered flags.

The clock ticks
a martyr taking steps
to her death.

A radiator boils
the heat of her body opens
with no one to hold her close.

The Last Day of the Year

Today,
I see a psychologist
and prepare
for bone marrow transplant.

Later,
I eat pizza
and dream of Italy.

Europe is a continent away
from stem cells
or stems of daisies.

I can't travel
and most bouquets
are out of season.

Thou Shall Not Lie Over Fried Fish

At the best biker joint
seafood joint
this side of Hazleton
where silver shrimp
is a quarter
on Thursday nights.

Oyster proclaims pheromones
clams ooze with butter
You tell
the story of a harpist
who Edna St. Vincent
might like to hear
playing for him

in Berlin bedrooms
where sirens capture
wrapped in chords in cords
and you did not perish.

Now, here you are,
muttering German
in a biker crab joint.
You cut batter dipped fish
with a black plastic
fork and knife.

The jukebox features
Skynard and Journey.
The featured beer is Budweiser.
For another quarter,
you can hear *Free Bird*

again and again and again.
He asks about
my sex escapades
I can't stomach
another bite
of badly spoken German
and rancid cocktail sauce.

I just spit out
the ultimate male fantasy.
I have my own siren
and what goes better
with crustacean
than two females together.

His eyes pop out
like a lobster
the instant before
boiled water pours
and scalds.

In The Room With No Light

She writes
And shivers by the window
As air hibernates
Along the cracks.
She wonders why
The wind's sleep
Is so cold.
Her hands type rest.
Nothing to do
But look for comfort
Against this hard shove of snow.

Volcano Gal

I don't move
like the tectonic plates
of Mt. St. Helen's volcano
an orchestrated chorus
of lava and ash.

They work together
to cool off an earth
from the sweaty operas
of millions of temper tantrums
a year.

The baritone's the ash
who climbs to the bottom
of the mountain's register.
He doesn't want
to damage any homes,
just take the low part
of the song seriously.

After all,
someone has to keep harmony.

The lava has to be
in the center
because the core
of a volcano
can't be seen
without a diva
with a red cape

flaunting the high notes

full of heat,
but the critics say
she lacks passion.

She doesn't give
a shit
who she ruins.

And, where do I fit?
You might ask.

I watch this drama
play out on television
in a recliner
waiting for test results.

An Alto
out of practice
from high school chorus
trying to save my body
out of tune.

Beachcombing With Intensive Care

Today, the sun almost has life.
I go to work
tired
a little hungover.

In the hospital,
you wear
octopus tentacles of plugs and tubes
that grab for breath, for food,
but not life.

All those arms
of oxygen and monitors
poke to find sustenance
not a nearby starfish,
that fills the stomach
for more than a short time.

The mattress doesn't
have sand like the beach.
If it could only be the Cape,
where the sand falls
in between the toes.
Prayer is a strong statement
for what is soft and lingers
along the feet.

Can heaven hold a body
like the shore?

Here, there's only
edema's litany.
The swelling of the ankle
and the day
makes it difficult
to walk
under a sky of 100-watt bulbs
and the linoleum shore.

I haven't visited for a week.
I should call. I should buy a card.
Write a line or two about the ocean
and how the rogassa roses
dance in wind.

I just carry a beach bag of questions
a bathing suit of why
a peppermint striped umbrella
the burn of what happens
when we get too much sun.

Let Me Receive His Body Whole

The Immaculate Hearts say
fold your hands
in reverence
to the Blessed Sacrament.

Receive Eucharist, girls.
Listen to the vocation
calling you
to a life for God.

The nuns forget
Mary Magdeline
washed Jesus's feet.

She is the first priest
anointing Christ's toes
with oils and kindness and perfume
wiping dirt and sand
with long brown hair
the strands of tangled imperfection.

Improvise

She's a woman
who french kisses blues
into a microphone.
Her tongue climbs
and each note
pumps breath
like that moment
right before orgasm.

At 4 AM, she's a girl
without words.
Her red hair collapses
under Aqua Net's weight.
Rain haunts her black umbrella
and plays on her silk dress.
The one she wears
dry cleaning after dry cleaning.

She grabs a taxi to her studio.
She taps ivory pumps
until the floor notices her.
Before sleep, she sips shiraz.
The wine stains her mouth purple.
She carries her glass
into the bathroom
and washes off
the makeup
window dressing her face.

Then, she walks to the bedroom.
She slips out of her dress.
She slips into skin's elegance
and climbs into bed.
Her hands finger jazz
and improvise happiness
between her legs.

A Little Death

At Nay Aug Zoo,
snakes hiss messages
and don't look
for an escape
from the ugly.

These creatures on wooden logs
craft insects into art.
Pursued tongues maim best.

Turn on the computer.
Turn off touch. Turn
off the TV.
Turn off consequence.

Pack groceries
with paper
inside plastic.
Wrap extra pennies.
Protect change falling
from pockets.
Avoid slithering around,
most of the time.

Putting Down Roots

Marilyn,
when John prompts you
to wear a blonde wig
and mirror Jackie,
it's the sliding of Mr. President
against a bubble-headed
movie goddess.

He makes a poor country chick
into an ambassador's daughter.
In bed, Marilyn speaks French.
Recites Millay.
Bears the name Bouvier.

Am I like
washed up Hollywood starlets
who think glamour
calls you to wear
dyed blonde and a tight sequined gown?

I'll settle down
and dress only in a Mardi Gras mask
with black plumage.
Bird-like, without the wigs.
I let him
carry the whip
the stiff and hard rope
almost worth remembering.

For first prize in makeout heaven,
He awards me with his mom's rosary.
He adds drama
casting Christ and leather together
handcuffs and hallowed be thy name.

Adolcha

What did this place offer you, Adolcha?
or Ethel
to the Italian neighbors
who couldn't pronounce
your name in Polish.

Your blue ribbon prize
a white house in a small neighborhood
and a guy who hit you.
Four kids who had to be
in Catholic school.

You were a homemaker,
wishing you stayed a secretary
in Washington.

In D.C.,
you typed away
from 10 brothers and sisters.
You danced
with soldiers at U.S.O. dances.
You planned your way
to the Foreign Legion
You sent
money back home.
Your only luxury
one big plate of roast beef
and mashed potatoes
on Sundays.

Single and liberated
before mom called you back to Scranton.

She brought you back
to this no wax floor
this chance to play a mother
this bartender husband
this beauty, and all of this,
all of this.

The Fall

She, this river,
is the only fallen woman.

She sorrows for us
and the short stay

of our temporary warm.
I sift sand

through hands
hoping to keep

the language of our February
legible.

I keep the small grains
close

because spring
reads different

then my company
in your story.

Shamrocks, Anyone?

I am so Scranton.
She says
with one eye
looking down

at the Celtic cross tattoo
on her arm.

She smiles
wanders through
green lined
downtown streets
adorned in perpetual memory
of St. Patrick's Day.

This city
a shit faced brunette
blacking out
at the very mention
of her name.

Unanswered

I wait for the phone to ring.
not for a boyfriend or a boy friend
but a doctor's call —
and his announcement
of my body's damage.

A fender bender of sickness
the spark that flies
from the bumper cars
three times.

I am a hit and run of no touch.
I am high school poetry.
Vocabulary that stays away
from:
nebulous and copulation.

I cop a plea for sleep
or maybe dreams
a prescription of comfort
for empty hands.

Blue

I go to your grave,
all the reassurance of dirt
scolding me I shouldn't complain
about my job
or the fact my hair is turning gray
but I see the shade of white
just the same.

When I come,
you spread out earth
and welcome me like a old friend.
I turn over soil
and put in geraniums.
I give you the latest news
on my new boyfriend.

I'd bring roses
but I pay too much attention
to the thorns.

I kill Christmas cactuses.
In fact, you know the murder
took place
because you left me
in charge of watering
those last days.

I failed you and the plants.

I had to go to the bar.
Our bed was the tundra.
How did you stay warm
if I couldn't?
I shut off your dying
like a lamp.

Staccato

The sleeping woman
finds comfort
in her snores
not her smile.

The Less Than Five Minute Vacation

Breakfast in Vienna
tastes best
if I prepare
the mix as espresso
a buzz and a shock
poured into
a demaitasse and drunk.

Because I live alone,
I pretend its strong coffee.
Saturate the beans
in Vienna's landscape
with the comfort
of water
dripping down.

A kind of European downpour
almost steady
but not enough rain
to step in
or make puddles.

My eggs and toast
should be accompanied
by a postcard of Europe
saying:

"Having a blast visiting Mozart's home."

What if I won't travel
beyond the kitchen
thoughts of Austria

and exotic roasts
Just that —

And me, the sender and the receiver
writing in soaked brown grains
along the edge
of a mug that doesn't move farther
than the cabinet, the table, the sink.

Loosening My Grip (Polished)

We watch
some animated French cartoon
in Kirby's Art Deco Theatre.

Is this what
"that"
should be
the greasy indecision
rising up my stockings
to the thigh.

"Yes," I answer.
You rub my hand
with your fingertips.
I bubble more ferocious
than vegetable oil
martyring a pound
of diner fries.
I cook in the lard
I know
will kill me.

In plush violet seats
our fingers move
where pulses connect.
I discover
your strongest pulse
a pinball bouncing
with one million nerve endings
and my nerves end there.

Our hands are moving pictures
while the characters mutter
something profound.
I can't say what
what can I say?

You hold my left hand
the whole time
and fingers tango
graceful and violent
along your black jeans
with the zipper pulled down
just enough.

The rain falls outside.
The downpour pelts
inside your pants
drenched
and not ready to dry.

A Kiss Before I Go

In the nursing home,
her lips pucker
as if to say
she doesn't have teeth.

Her tongue's tired
if she could receive
one more kiss
her mouth would manage
to purse and pucker up.

There is a connection between two muscles
whose meeting jabs more in one round
than a whole fight of the pelvis's violence.

"Men are too heavy."
she says
as she reclines
in her oversized chair

I believe.

Christmas Cactus

The cactus is afraid
to make the commitment
to blossom.

Unwed
and not engaged
The leaves stay green
and wait to blossom pink
while no one's looking.

They are shy bridesmaids
at the altar
fixing the train
on the bride's gown
while the ruffles
on their dresses
wrinkle ever so slightly.

Airports Are For Flying
(*for Erin Moreken*)

She picks up skirts and sweaters
and Billie Holiday's *Lady In Satin*.
She throws suitcases and bags
in the car; and crushes
a one way ticket to New Orleans
in her hand.

She has no girlfriend
to kiss under June's deluge.

She unloads yellow slips
and green paisley dresses.
Her fabric longs for place here;
not the cruel Louisiana heat.
Vintage clothes don't do travel much....

This isn't a Saturday matinee.
She isn't Ingrid Bergman
going away
Casablanca style
with the glory
of MGM
black and white goodbyes.

In Avoca's one terminal,
she pushes away
the grainy afternoon
with her brown hair.
She breaks the latch
on a black umbrella.
Summer won't lift

the chronic rain
landing as she flies away.

Swallowing Myth

I am Echo
the goddess whose
voice quakes in the earth

of Narcissus's words.
Our mythology cooks
like two summer picnic

pigs in a blanket.
Warring countries
who wrap

in the peace treaty
of cabbage and noodles
and sign with grease.

Lexicon

In the this
before we kiss,
I wonder what
heals us enough

to listen to our tongues
and pull lips together
in some unspoken vernacular.

We smooch with the intention
of 1,000 saints and prostitutes
between our teeth.

We write through longing
that stumbles from
centuries of minutes.

Without language,
what dictionaries
we conjure!

Misfit

When I was seven,
I remember trips to Woolworth's
and this pink blouse with gold stripes.
I prayed it would fit
because to have something new
is precious.

I can still see those puffy sleeves
and those stripes of gold
laid into the fabric
like a lover that doesn't belong
in bed
after morning.

Now, I wish for smaller gifts
hoping for
the said puffy shirt again.
I need to display this trophy
to more
than the elongated universe
of the mirror.

But,
disease is the dress
that doesn't fit.
I keep putting it on
and it doesn't wear out.

I'd love to get that
gaudy pink back.
I'd trade that blouse
for the dress I'm forced
to display.

I'd parade through the five and dime.
Proclaim the horrendous charm
of this shirt
throughout the coffee shop
and in the checkout lines.

Permanent press
without the bereavement and grief
of the little black number
I'm forced to wear
every goddamned day.

Acceptance

I carry sorrow
like a long married couple
who dances their way
through small talk.

I don't know what
the physicians will do next.
My sisters are
bone marrow matches.

The doctors state
the growth
in my chest
needs more time
to bloom
before flowering.

I want the call
of marrow
to come soon
arrive at my doorstep
in some wrapped package
I didn't expect.

Sayonara

Saying goodbye is never easy.
Qualify the word never
and question why
I put it in a sentence.

Wind passes
through insulation
and rattles the window;
at least
the breeze has someone to hold.

The winter
is just not good
with hellos or making friends.

You leave the trees
with a white sugar coating
I can't eat.

What good is sugar
if I can't use it
to mellow
my coffee or tea?

Sunday Morning

I always wanted to be
the character in
Wallace Steven's
Sunday Morning.

I could drink tea
and eat oranges daintily.

Contemplate
philosophy or art
or heaven or
a heavenly bird's flight.

Instead, my waking up
consists of wondering how bad
the pain in my chest might be
or do I have enough money
or where in the hell
my cell phone is located
at the present moment.

I write this poem
for those of us
who don't read
the New York Times
after sunrise
whose wake up call
consists of burned Wonder Bread toast
and orange juice from concentrate.

Memorial Day For Mice

The mouse who crawls up
the drain
into the shower
is a martyr.

My answer
to his need
for a quickie
is a swift hit
with the nearest weapon:
a toilet brush.

I grab the
bathroom death accoutrement
because every girl
must protect herself
from unwanted visitors.

He wants to jerk off
by practicing his foot fetish.
I have to punish him somehow.
He sees the cellulite on my thighs.
The stretch marks expand
across my stomach.

On this Route 66 of skin
you drive past California
swim through the Pacific Ocean
and land in an igloo
in Alaska.

No slight swoosh of tail
will tell
where the stubble on my knee
congregates like teenagers
at the mall.

I silence the one man
who appreciates
all this baby powdered ugliness.
I kill
what saves.

For Barbaro And St. Jude's Kids

Kentucky Derby winners
have luck
and four legs
but God doesn't
make promises
for boys and girls
walking on two.

On my birthday,
Barbaro gets sent to pasture.
I watch a special
on kids
from St. Jude's hospital.

Barbaro's legs shatter.
The universe cracks
every good thing
that's not damaged.
Horses can't be tender
after the fall.

Barbaro got
the top veterinarian
to care
for hooves
that collapsed under
the weight of a jockey
and expectation.

Those kids
are bridled
with more than broken legs.
They trip on
neuroblastoma.
These diseases should be
distant countries.
The language is so ugly to the lips.

How are a horse and a child different?
His mane stays combed to perfection.
Those kids just get bald
somewhere between needle sticks and the last kiss.

Violets For Your Furs

I visit your ashes
that grace an urn
like the vases
we stuffed with tulips
stolen from St. Mary's Church.

Piano keys
struggle along
to Billie Holiday.

These keys
trickle and drip.
I remember chasing you
up and down the cellar stairs
cups of tea with two spoons of sugar
the way you held your cigarette
pointing the tip toward sky
flicking each black speck
in the ashtray
a nicotine masterpiece.

I burn in the leftover smoke
of sleep
that trembles in air.
I'd place a violet in my hair
but these flowers are small
and easy to forget.

Novena For The Descendants of Immigrants Who Built The Church

Listen, I am damned.
On St. Ann's Feast Day,
I went down on a guy
and laid my hands on
Mary's mother's statue.

Touch gives dementia of flesh
where heaven doesn't throb
or ache
like arthritis before rain.

My terminal
lungs breathe make me better intentions.

When Ann doesn't answer,
kindness slips between
the spaces of rosary beads.
Joyful and sorrowful mysteries
connect in a thin strand of twine.

On Watch

I squint to see the clouds.
I look at the anxiety
of their gray approach.
They worry, too.
I think about the ache

under my breastbone.
The doctors take care
of viewing it for me.
I run out of images.
What is an hour without

a sip of Earl Gray
test results
a good line for a poem?

I don't know about
the day after tomorrow.
The sky is a soliloquy
with no words.

Splinter

When I was ten,
I got a nail
from the tool storage bin
stuck in my foot.

My mom thought
I would need
a tetanus shot.
The blood was afraid
of the air
and stopped like
a car at a red light
A bandaid ended fear.

Now, though,
this is not
the season for faith.
This is the time
to listen for snow.

Home Movie

Two people on the living room carpet.
The light turns down
just enough.

Some movie gets popped into the DVD.
Annie Hall for her.
A Fistful of Dollars for him.
Toes stick out
from under the comforter.

Popcorn escapes from its cocoon
in the microwave.

One girl unravels like yarn
into his arms.
One guy touches her cheek
with his hands.

Then, one guy and one girl
hibernate on a floor
that creaks with the hardwood
of good conversation.

He wants this to be
his film for everyday.
Her face burrowed into his chest.
But, there are chores to finish
and there is always morning.

Blue Tuesday

The sky is azure.
I am blue Tuesday
not for the leaves
that trace tree's fingerprints
along the ground
but for love
the clever and undefined abstraction
caught in the first storm
that's supposed
to land tomorrow.

The flakes will make
their high school prom
toward ground.
The snow lives
as not quite popular girls
in bad ruffled lame' dresses
while the cars run over
their almost beauty.

I take this time
before winter
and mourn
before the sky
readies its breath
and the clouds exhale
their white tragedies.

Thin Skinned

I want to love my skin
like tissue paper
before you open
the birthday present.
I haven't received this gift.
It is either fat or steroids
that makes me look like a freak.

I regret the way
my body has morphed
from plump to skinny
skinny to obese
without a choice.

I have only
the itchiness of flesh
to remind me
The bully Hodgkin's hangs out
at the swimming pool
a kid kicked out
of summer school
ready to jump into my body
and dive in.

Angels Don't Idolize Joan Crawford (or her drawn in eyebrows)

Guardian angels only like
the right shoulders.

I hold on to an angel
who wears a submissive face.
as if she could be a poor graduate student
and I could be a cheap ceramic.

There can be no difference
in the exchange of sorrow
whether from a not quite porcelain angel
or from a girl on the verge of flight
not sure how to hang her wings
and find the Hollywood version of death,
Complete with fluffy white clouds.

Your goodbye angel
comes with another
Cracker Jack Prize.
A coffee table on ancient movie starlets.
Knick knack guardian angels
eavesdrop for gossip.
of Joan Crawford's downfall
from *Mommie Dearest* to *Baby Jane*.

She lost the MGM contract.
She couldn't strangle herself
with wire or plastic hangers.
She could live forever
As *Mildred Pierce*.

A bucolic housewife
guarding her children
with arms circling
like halos full
of golden devotion.
She failed the screen test of pretty.
I flunked pretty, too.

The Salvation Of Fishnets

I scheme to be a fisher of men.
I hook a few holy hours
from a just engaged man
happy for the bait.

I want you.
want has a short A
a hunger to hold
crunched up stockings
to clutch bent and spread legs
happy-go-lucky breasts
and hung over bones.

The A
is the one letter
We can't always sound out
to read.

I need you.
Need jumps like a sheep
a psalm shorn of EE's
without a shepherd
to lead the flock home.

Loosening My Grip (Raw)

I let you feel me up
watching a French cartoon
in an Art Deco theatre.
I allow the greasy indecision
of your fingers rising up
my stockings to the thigh.
I bubble more ferocious
than vegetable oil martyring
a pound of diner fries;
cooking in the heat
I know will kill me.

Our fingers move
where pulses connect
and I discover your strongest pulse
a pinball bouncing
with one million nerve endings
and my nerves always end there.

As animated characters flash along the screen,
our hands are moving pictures,
because you hold
my left hand and fingers tango
graceful and violent
along your black jeans
with the zipper pulled up
just enough
playing in violet plush seats
waiting to get caught
to get thrown into the street.

We reel in the thrill
of the usher's flashlight.
His high beams almost careen
into our night.
The rain falls outside
but a downpour pelts
below your belt
under my skirt
drenched and is never
ready to dry.

Te Quiero

Laboranti's on a Saturday night
a birthday party
Midnight for Portugal
in the back of this bar
about the size of a bedroom.

Boas fly.
The host, Melck,
in silver wigs and feathers
to Portuguese dance music
I tether to the trance
and float on the high of rhythm.

He whips his guests in tight vinyl
plays dominatrix
as double DD strippers
celebrate divinity in bikinis
bend into sainthood
leather thongs not constricting skin.

Praise be the breast and the buttocks.
Woman slipping tongue to woman.
Men necking with men.
Girls grabbing the small
Of a boyfriend's back.

This Mardi Gras lifts me away.
I flash for one strand
of dollar store bangles
dripping in plastic
Purple beads become currency.

Spanish legs tap
as easy as each case of beer.
Collide in the dancer's g string.
One dollar bills bulge
and these riches always come.

L and Y

She looks out the window.

Ice is her slippery audience.
How did her life's comet
trail into poetic lines
as predictable as
smudged windows on glass?

She hums to herself.
and sits at the typewriter.
She wonders how she
can use the word lonely

without the keys
getting stuck
on the "l" or "y".

Surrender, Spring

Bring me
the good news
of melted snow
on a silver platter.

If the spring
can take away anything,
this would be the start
of lilacs and goldenrod and delight.

Instead, machine gun prayers
fire from the mouth of doctors.
They play rifle practice
through my veins.

I am too young
to be holding rosary beads
in my crossed, unmoving hands.

Devil Vs. Angel

The haloes of angels
have given up their luster
the angles of haloes are bent
and without shine.

The devil is polished and refined.
He withstands tornadoes
bikini blondes
category five winds
and the last gasp before orgasm.
He never loses at chess, either.

Angels want so much
to be the creature
who gives up the wings
and join the human body
one way or the other.
whether naked or under the covers.

They think it's lovely
that we die and live and live and die
all in the same bed.

However,
The devil is more careful.
He considers what happens
when one has to get up
when one can't stay
for a moment longer
when one must get dressed and leave
one must let out secrets
of who slept with whom.

Angels are such fools.
They profess to a God
who could sever their feathers
in an instant.

They take the Lear Jet
of their wings
and divide time
between the East and West coasts.
Their frequent flier miles
get less and less each year.

The devil isn't so wishy washy.
He doesn't need menial help.
He does the job
because he doesn't fall for distraction.
He mingles among the living
and keeps a short distance.

Alive?

What can I do but write?
Not focusing on all the beers
I don't drink anymore.

It's all relative, beloved,
The doctor doesn't care
And neither
does the nurse, really.

What comfort can they offer?
A pain pill, a dish of ice cream?
Time moves on.
Young movie stars die.

While I hurt
My body preserved by loss
as the sun births her rays
through a winter sky.

Why Finger Puppet Nuns Are Best To Clutch During Emergency Landings

The pilot comes on the speaker.
We don't have landing gear.
We will be landing quickly.
Don't be alarmed by fire engines.
Make sure there's nothing under your feet.
Secure your seat belt, please.

In my purse
a finger puppet nun
with lips pursued
in singing God's chorus.

She was not baptized.
How can she die
when she had no anointing
with holy water
and salvation of a name?

I baptize you, Sister What?
What is the best nomenclature
for a finger puppet nun?
She will only be asked once
before the plane descends.

Mary, too predictable.
Mabel, too 1950's.
I use the letter M
as a frame of reference.
The Catholic tradition of every sister
attaching the Virgin Mary as a prefix
to the name her mother gave her

after the drugs wore off.
Is this what having a child is like?
This constant need to reassure
to make a place
when this claustrophobic plane
might explode into eternal with one puff.

She should be Colette.
the dichotomy
of naming her
Colette, of risqué writer fame,
or St. Colette
founder of the Poor Clares
friend of St. Francis.

All this talk of names
while our plane falls.
This newly professed
may be the closest
I get to a kid.
My unknown entity
floating through space.

I choose Madame St. Colette
of The Alphabetically Categorized Holy Rollers.
and Colette's risque novel's fame.

Madame St. Colette
Of the lonely Madonna drag queens.
Pray for us.
Of what God intended to be straight
Pray for us.
Of the strippers that are more than T and A
Pray for us.

Of the in the closet feminists
Pray for us.
Of all those in the closet
Pray for us,

Of the newly divorced
Forgive us.
Of the civilly united
Forgive us,
Of the married and not unhappy
Forgive us.
Of the adulterers
Forgive us.

Of the skaters, punks, nerds and Goths
Save us.
Of the all the kids who got pushed into lockers
Save us.
Of the smalltown blue collar worker
Save us.

Of the starving
Redeem us.

Of the beautifully old and the beautifully odd
Miserere nobis.
Of the weekend drinkers and brown bag winos
Miserere nobis.

Of the survivors of AIDS,
Dona nobis pacem.
Of the love and lust seekers
Dona nobis pacem.
Of the the always alone

Dona nobis pacem.

Of the unknown writers
Pray.
Redeem.
Save.
Forgive.
Have mercy.
Grant us peace.

The stewardess says
"We've landed safely."
Please remain seated
with seat belts fastened
until the plane
makes a complete stop.

May Be

I may be the girl twirling
     on a swivel chair
          drinking coke and cherry juice.

The chick sipping cosmos
     one hand on the glass
          one hand in a would be could be partner's lap.

His tie and her skirt her tie and his skirt
Her skirt and her skirt his tie and his tie

The elderly lady
     puts canned peas away
          in a brown kitchen counter.

One by one
until sealed containers
can't be stacked
any closer.

The Disease Of Waiting

We weren't prepared for nights together
alone in hospital rooms
where the nurse pulled out a cot
for you to sleep on
and sex sleeps as rare as the word zylophone
in everyday vocabulary.

We couldn't prophesy
the mouth infections, the kidney infections
the ear infections.
Isaiah announcing Christ
and His mountain of antibiotics.

I didn't think you'd stay.
After all,
We only dated for six months.
What did you owe me?
There is no poetry
or the expectation of what might arrive.
A recurrence or a remission.
maybe radiation--
A Fellini film gone chemical.

With an extra hour of day,
I salvage these minutes
how I will do
in the office party of chemo
in recliners you can tilt back to rest.
infusing life or the imitation of.

On the wall,
1,000 piece puzzles of farms

hang framed
as Barbara Walters
talks about Hillary Clinton
and Barack Obama
and who will be elected.

After the election news,
A kid on a soap opera
talks about
getting a bone marrow transplant.
His thick black hair
slathered with gel.

He finds his match,
While we get blood or shots or medicine
waiting,
waiting for the last drip.
the last, drip.
The drip that will make us last.

May I Now Pronounce You

The wedding reception was held in the backyard.
among the chickens whose heads
got spared for the day
because of the festivities.
Here, a fiddle player dangled polkas
along his bow.
like a man ready to jump off the bridge
and take the dive
without considering consequence.

Each note
closer to the staccato of disaster.
He played as if this America
was an Eastern Europe of South Sixth Ave.
Backyard rooster and weeds
homemade booze and strappin' Ukrainan and Polish
families
caught in the indigestion
of ghumpkis and vodka.

In 1944,
She was 27.
Back from Washington,
she worked at the railroad station.
and talked about
going back to D.C.

Mike and Adeline
eyed each other
Since they swimmed together as teenagers
in the West Side pool.
He prided himself as the bully.

She prided herself lanky with small tits.
Once, he saved her from going under
when she forgot to hold her breath
so she had to say *I do*.

What other choice
does one have
going under the water slow?
Smalltowns do this.
You have to tread water
when the air in your lungs
doesn't exhale all
of the carbon dioxide.

But, oh, the peace of the poison
the truth of the lack of oxygen
moves close to the heart's precipice.
She'd like to see how
the bottom of the pool feels
and stay there.

Before the wedding cake,
the Ukrainan men said,
Mike shouldn't have left
his mom Catherine.
His mother wanted Adeline to promise
the first born child
to her care.

The fiddler continued
as the coal miners fought
and made black and blue bruises.
The punches came.
The chickens cackled in their cages.

The booze oozed from dislocated noses.
Such was the reception of Michael and Adeline.

Adeline slept at home that night.
The men had the chance to fight
above the dirt.
After all, the mines sired close spaces.
No room to throw a proper left hook
only time to use a pick ax
and whittle away all the black.

Grandma,
You looked lovely
in the wedding gown.
Cinched in waist, tall and longing.
that night,
Did you sleep in all that white?
Did you place the dress
by the bedside?
Wonder how the lace and sequins
held you so well?
Somehow, the dress looked better
on the dresser
laid out
as careful as the dead.

In Vogue

My bra straps fall down all the time.
It's just a habit they have.
Don't ask them why
or question they're motive
for the behavior.
My legs leave
leftover stubble like a bad friend
who just won't stop calling.

I don't discuss granny panties.
This is an area of study
I won't involve myself in.
My clothes are too big on me.
I float around in sweat pants
when I should be wearing trousers..

Ask anyone:
I grovel to have a dark blue denim jeans
the ones with the tapered legs
with enough space to fit a leather boot
stomping around
for the whole city of Scranton to see.

Almost the time of Kennedy's stay in office,
1000 days, I've been sick.
so I'm stuck
with these faux pais of fashion
around my body
and only one pair of sneakers…

I sit in the accessory of a wheelchair
They don't make leopard print arm rests.

No place for a purse
in this outfit.
The wheels are enough to hold on to.
We won't even mention the hospital gown.
I picture a brand new style with sequins and feathers.
who says you have to be ill
and unstylish.

It's ridiculous to be ugly.
Forgive me,
But I'm not done
with sensuous yet.

Mea Culpa

In 8th grade,
I was a disgrace
when Sr. Carol said
It was *my fault*
that the kids made fun of me.

After all,
She told my parents,
She's overweight and has stubbly legs.
Her knee socks
don't have enough elastic
to stay up to the knee.
She keeps getting
these horrible tight perms.
Why don't you let her hair
grow straight?

In high school,
one of the cheerleaders, Melissa,
lied and shouted
she was sick with leukemia
than made an ass out of me
by proclaiming it was false
on Senior Day.

I recall
how sorry I felt
believing it true.
Now, no one in my high school
remembers me.
except if I had my name
in the bridal section or the obituary section.

Take your pick.

On the eves of my 20th reunion,
Anger enlarges my hips
like all the pleats in my uniform skirt
all that scratchy wool and plaid
was hard to fit in to.

These skirts are still
as stiff as starch now.
I can't take it off.
Be comfortable.
I fear the detention of closed eyes
with pennies underneath.
I have the fear of getting fat
and having too small curl permanents.

The horror of those peter pan collars
white and ironed.
The creases as perpetual
as votive candles
humble but burning.

Blue Note

Dawn waits as dark exalts still air.
Crickets sing the last standards
of forgotten August
remembered September.
Late night jazz melodies
play on a transistor radio.

Leaves change, though.
Love, she remembers
is the space between seasons
when his fingers
brush her hands
right before sleep.
She doesn't want to leave
and hesitates as she walks out
the kitchen door.

One Minute Stand

Two computers away,
I can't see your eyes.
I can see the water colored liars.

But the truth is told
in the pupil
The black dot
in the middle that sees.

How can I bait you into belief
I do write a decent love poem
or two.

You plop your black shoes
on the desk.
I walk into what
I want to picture.

Far from this
instant message trance
I sit in your kitchen.

You glance across
the table
and I sip myself
into that first coffee.

Watch you untangle
your brown hair
then wash your hands
and bite into a peach.

Until the juice drips
until we only
exchange emails.

Vowels and consonants
cooked in web-bed space.
We tangle in talk
of Neruda's sonnets.

Initiate each key
stroke as if tango
dips in 12 point type.

How easy I squeeze
into pink stilettos
when the spike points
straight at the screen.

Frostbite

You scrape off the car before work
trample into it, put on your hat
dust off the snow as ice bitters the tongue.
You shatter air with every breath.
My red strands of air print
an alphabet along your down comforter.
As I roll over, I hear you pick up your keys,
struggle with your boots and close the door.
I take residence in December.
Frost away another hour.
Bite my life to spring.

Writers Block or How To Stop Writing Poems About A Lover Whose Gone

I have to climb
a Mt. Kilamanjaro of steps
to get to the poetry reading.

I say I don't believe
in writer's block.
I am just in a elderly facility
and the pricks from the insulin machine
are cruel lovers
knowing they hurt
but still insist on going in
just the same.

What poetry can be found here
in a box of a room
with a single bed
and not even a square inch
for another's fingers, toes.

I fail to think of a sentence
that might interest you
that might include you
in this nursing home
where the leaves outside
choose to change colors,
for minutes, maybe hours.

This quick fall allows winter
to blow in
and leave January
lounging along evergreens

waiting for their boyfriends
called icicles
to touch them
and give much welcome company.

I don't have such pleasure.
I listen to a man moan.
Watch families keep vigil of the dying.

I see you have a new girl
and a new book
while I crawl through the dictionary
find the word beloved
and pray it has a meaning.

Grace

She is the girl
between fall and winter
whose eyes wear
all kinds of weather
while a crucifix clings
to tulip wallpaper.
She lets these flowers
touch her.

This is a garden
she doesn't water or weed.
She puts out her hand
rubs the petals
against her lifeless grace.
She pulls up the covers
and tries to sleep.

A Miracle For A Wednesday

Forgive the stench of sentiment
to scrub the kitchen floor
fix the kitchen's flickering light
with no bulbs.

I am a working girl
who lives from paycheck to paycheck
who picks the dry skin
from her fingers
when she's nervous.

No one is that interested
in the epic of a girl
with eczema.

I should get some lotion
to soften the heels and feet.
All the places that get rough
and no one notices.

There's no soft spots
for the mind…

I get seconds of happiness
but can I have
the miracle of a day, maybe,
where the honesty of dawn
lasts well past morning.

The Alligators Crusade Against Cliché

I am too much
of a novice
for a brigade of alligators
around my canoe.

Somewhere in the Susquehanna
they trespass
through the swamps and bad weather
to find me with a fishing pole
waiting for trout or bass
or some kind of fish
you're supposed to catch.

And then the alligator says:
we can take away your boredom.
We will make you an atheist,
sexy. 120 pounds and 38 DD.
You will have a different Brad Pitt every night.
Transgress against the shit
of husbands, babies, and family.
Otherwise, I have to eat you.

With all those scales
and that big jaw near my legs,
I answer

Swallow me
reptile insurrectionist
for I'd rather be
trapped inside your mouth
in the slobber of your ordinary
than transformed on a shore

with a low cut sequined dress
and an empty fishing pole
to bring home.

Chew me up
in the violence
of your militant smile.
Let me join
the daily mass goers
the Altar and Rosary society ladies
who'd rather
the sharp cut of your incisors
then to deny like Peter
their lives.

I share the alligator's body
with the faithful.
Please forgive me, Dear Alligator,
but you have
A far too liberal
open leg policy.

You wouldn't
let me practice
the cliché of marriage
or allow me to make
Sunday turkey dinner
cooked just enough
not dry, just tender.

The Weight Of Patience

On a metal table
shiny as a silver ribbon
on a Christmas present,
I got my unwanted marks.
There was no penny candy here
no Swedish fish
that tug on loose teeth.

There was only
this laying down
this surrendering to a doctor
who relied on the color gray
to mark a body
whose knowledge of gray
could fill medical history.

What can I sacrifice
for a bright orange popsicle
the double magic
of two orange popsicles
on one stick?

The kind Mr. Mazzei
gave me
and my sister Tara
at the mom and pop shop
for 10 cents
after swimming
in my Grandma's backyard
above ground pool.

I can't complain.
I'm supposed to be getting better.
I'd like to shout fuck you
but I can't argue
with the painters
who stencil on my body
and paint my bones alive
so that I may see Spring
with a clear sky.

Still Life

The unfolding of ordinary
breathing makes us play a game of Tic Tac Toe.
Fill in the calendar.
Circles on the weekends.
Cross off Today.

A cross hangs quiet
on a cubicle bulletin board.
Two pieces of wood
are nothing but a brief remembrance
to connect.

Tuesday type.
Just work. Just business. Just finances.
A desk. An office.
Another tall building in New York.
Family pictures placed in silver frames.
They are the people who fire life
beyond 5 o'clock.

At 9:03,
A thousand alphabets speak
running down stairs
or flying out windows.

Hangman float in air.
Tie in a noose of flight.
No vowels to fill in the consonants
tumbling to earth.

This late summer morning
a photograph
blasting light into the negative.

Book II

Selections from:
Wear White and Grieve

Table of Contents

Book II

Publisher's Notes on Wear White And Grieve Selections:

2010 © by Jennifer Diskin

These poems were presented as a chapbook in 2010. The chapbook was printed on white paper, with a striking over image of a picture taken of a mannequin bride and groom pair in a store front. Since these poems I find as "genius poetry" and was printed on basic white paper with one red sheet of paper that folded to the front and back (and stapled together).

This collection would not be complete without 15 selections of poetry chosen by Jennifer's family from the iconic "Wear White And Grieve."

The original Acknowledgments of Wear White And Grieve are reprinted here:

2005- The Periodic Table For Mad Intellectuals, Marywood University, Mulberry Poet Installation of poetry and art.

April 2007 -Monet IN the Basement, Blue Dot Tattos Verses Tinkerbell Fairies, *Wicket Alice*, online journal.

Corset Alphabet, The Arc Of A Cry, Binghamton, NY, Fall 2007.

(Original cover photo of Wear White And Grieve) was done by Carla Reck.

Thanks to my Mom and Dad, Tara Fox, Leslie Clapp, Joe Weil, Lis Balise, Carla Reck, Jennifer Hill and Dan Waber.

Electric City

The Italian festival has the tents up.
The summer's over
except for cannoils and ziti and meatballs
The best I can do
is surrender
to homemade sauces and cheesecakes
all delights so sweet
you would think paradise is
right here on North Washington St. and Linden Ave.
right above the electric light of Scranton.

But, I eat my broccoli and shells alone.
Lemonade is very tart
when you have one straw
instead of two.

When I watch the babies in strollers,
a pregnant lady with her husband
a guy and girl walking hand in hand
I want their plates.

I want to skip this festival
and have my own backyard barbeque
complete with hamburgers and hot dogs
grilling away Labor Day
with a picnic
for the neighborhood kids and dogs.

This is life's history.
Dad hold's Mom's hand
sitting on lawn chairs
before it's time to get up

pack a lunch
and get ready for work
or school tomorrow…

Pull Down The Covers, Once More

Strike me a spell for my sorrow tonight
and you shall make me an upright woman.

Sing me a song with something
happy in the title and I might listen.

Go above rituals, the closing of our eyes
the saying of good night. Before the kiss

ends, I won't slip away from lips this time.
I won't move from such a simple offering.

Give me comfort and these hours
will move me away

from a cloud-filled destination. Excuse
me. I veer off when you asked if

I am like this. Or that.
Twilight intrudes too soon.

We read and nothing
but pages hold us anymore.

Under lying eyelids of dreams,
I stand

across the bar
from you. Just come

on to the gal with the red dress.
I like to dance.

Please, shimmy with me through
the glimmer of never.

Then, we can lay down and touch.
Touch and rest.

Flowers For Jennifer

My lymph nodes bloom
As plentiful as backyard peonies.
Each bulb bigger than the other.

Not Kennedy roses
In their quiet repose.
I let the medical doctor

Germinate me
In a greenhouse
Of biopsies and mourning light.

This planting season
Is very long.
Oh, lymphoma, you are perennial.

Three syllables beautiful
A white hybrid
All my own.

Walking, Alive and Well

The walls are white
in this bedroom
where we
attempt our own
separate suicides
but only dull butter knives
knick us open.

We cut skin
at least we don't bleed
and force our hands
to clean up
the mess we've made.

As if anyone would notice,
We finish living.
Our lone witness
a Sacred Heart statue
leaning against the dresser.

You are St. John
singing canticles
for the bride.

I am St. Theresa
sending roses
to the forlorn.

We aren't mystics, though,
just two souls scheming

for the eternal
as broken down cars
back rent
and long morning glances
remind us we can't stop.
…Not yet.

The Last Shall Be First

Outside an Adams Avenue bar,
(the least likeliest place)
you kiss me.
I don't know
if I screwed up the moment and afterwards
because this time I must win.

I don't want a repeat
of the St. Pat's Spelling Bee
in the school auditorium
sharing the stage
with Dina Murray
the cheerleader/brain and future accountant.
(There is a difference between brains and nerds.)

The coveted trophy
and trip to the University of Scranton
for the city bee
was all I desired.
What chance did I have?

Dina could wear her skirts short;
her knee socks pulled up high.
I preferred to wear my skirts long.
My knee socks met my skirt.
No boy would consider
looking underneath.

Since I didn't have
Chad Doherty's hand to hold,
I needed the comfort of all
that plated trophy offered.

Sr. Joan said,
"Jennifer, spell the word sophistry."

I knew the meaning:
One who is good at pretending.

I picked on a zit
and pushed up my glasses
three times
before I gave my answer.

"S-O-P-H-E-S-T-R-Y," I said.
"That's wrong. Please sit down."

"S-O-P-H-I-S-T-R-Y."
"Correct, wonderful, my dear."

Dina spoke the letters
as if she had completed heart bypass surgery.
While she flipped her curly locks,
she gave the guard
from the basketball team
a resurrection in his pants.
She has gotten to first base
and the chance to go to the
Scripps/Howard Spelling Bee.

I couldn't wait to get to lunch
to wander around
the old oak tree in the playground.
Alone.

Almost 20 years later,
I need something

that doesn't require
a contest
and the chance to lose.

I want the trophy
to be his lips
not sprayed with gold
but a red flame
containing the fire
of the Holy Spirt.
Wisdom sparked on the tongue
blazing.

Monet In The Basement

A poet is supposed to be angry.
A woman poet at least.
But she doesn't speak.
She believes in the litany
Of laundry, unwanted celibacy,
More celery in the chicken soup.

Her forty hour a life job
As comfortable as elastic jeans
The 9.99 special, well,
Promises to fit.
She forces herself to suck in.
She is as near to skinny
As Pluto is to earth.

She gets fat
Because he trashed his birthday gift.
A book on Impressionist Art.
Another coffee table present
He flips through and throws
In a drawer.

He must find a place for this present.
He won't put the book in
His underwear drawer.
He doesn't want
Water lilies growing
Below boxers and argyle socks.

He's tired of Impressionists.
Monet sees flowers as splashes
Of purple and pink.

No better than kindergarden smudges
Along the beige refrigerator
Banana and apple magnets
Read to slip
At the force of attraction.

He thrives best with earth tones.
Brown and green.
He waters spider plants and ivy.
He cares for house plants well.

She wishes Giverny,
Monet's Garden,
But this is Scranton.
She can't expect him to know
Impressionists play with imagined reflections.
Using primary colors instead of dirt.

She should be mad.
She should not use
The word should.
Her heart is a tickertape
Printing out silent minuses.
She subtracts 2-1=1.
Math as nothing
To do with impressionists.

She is a poet, second.
A woman, first.
She may find the right lipstick.
She may find the right size.
She will balance the scale
When she believes in
More than numbers.

Suffering For The Right Line

Yeah, Ted Hughes is someone to idolize.
Sylvia died in a drafty house
with little heat
from the thermostat
or Ted's hands.

She couldn't handle the kids,
She was crazy, the reader says.
If you had two children,
and a husband
who bedded other intellectual cunts
I might act the same way, too.

Most male writers
abandon the wife
for a place
in the literary canon
a cute trophy wife
on his arm for awhile.

Sylvia held Ted
a pen in her hand
unhappy with how fast
the ink dries.

Matting is one quick thrust
of penetrating what
involves the heart.

The tight fist
of a handsome alphabet hurts
long after the first punch.

Wear White And Grieve

I got a new cell phone.
with a *Sex and the City* ring.
a kitschy melody
I won't switch for *Pachelbel's Canon*.

We adore hipsters
and drink in pop culture
like beer on draft.

I long for classic novels
where gentle men
pulled out chairs
until ladies
found a comfortable place.

Now, everything stops.
Obituaries are printed online.
The dead deleted
with one swift click.

We worry about having car keys.
have intercourse at lunch,
work fifty hours with no break.

We revisit the quickie
for one minute
because two minutes
makes the moment pop less
and no fun to gossip about.

How does
the post modern couple
document hope?
I can't retrieve
The creak
my hardwood floors make
as you get up from bed
and put on your pants
Pull up one leg
then another.

For Whom It May Concern, Poppies

Before you, reader,
Have rubbed away the rust of sleep,
we touch.
Yes, ambivalent and cautious, at best,
while a nightingale
who makes
disapproval sound lyrical
or, at the very least, on key.

They fill in the blank lovemaking
and accept a wake up call with no frills.
He leaves on the tube socks with red stripes.
She lets her underwear squirm along ankles
and not on the floor.
Thank God some erotica includes the flaws.

These are two nerds who concentrate during chess,
who talk about auctions and books
who appreciate knick knacks and cracked spines. (first
edition hardcovers)
Yes, careful student of literature,
they may be the characters you thumb over
without thinking
because the story is too boring
for a Sunday newspaper morning
full of human interest articles
about 100 year old grandmothers
that credit long life to macramé
the occasional nip of brandy
and strict belief in family.

She doesn't talk about a day
mixed with flowers.

These days existed once for this widow
but filler pieces talk about generalities
not what position her daughter was conceived in
or where her husband's finger felt best,
just dress factories and sacrifice
all the hard work
that is more important that the details.

Think about your greatest sex
the most superlative EST ending.
Be honest from start to finish.
Don't give the girl a bustier.
Give her more than an ample stomach
and a bra that doesn't match her panties,
all the imperfection of light against
the beginning wrinkles on her face.
Give him a slight paunch, grey hair,
a want for getting jerked off
instead of coming inside.

Please, make your own vocabulary for the day.
Use two syllables, not one. You know
even dorks get some now and then.
To whomever scans these lines, I say
take into account a protagonist who doesn't drink coffee
but brews a cup filled with the additions
of chocolate milk (that's all he has) and brown sugar.
The caffeine is sweeter than what
She's used to this early.
Picture another cup, small talk,
And a walk before work.

Invent a reason for her staying the night.
Make her spit out awkward but caring dialogue
something as basic as the phrase,
I like your poppies.
For a minute,
allow him to brag about his horticulture skills.
Dear Reader,
remember the gratitude
of one who turns over the soil
and digs every year.
Don't deny this male and female
the orange grace of tissue paper flowers
or the black center of mourning.
Plant this couple into a garden
with plenty of perennials.
Some will bloom. Some won't.
You decide.

Geisha Is Not Part Of The Local Dialect

Geishas live in the pale truth of the face.
These so-much-better than Miss Americas
massage a man's feet and discuss haiku
before the first meeting of lips.

When I don't put on my glasses,
the valley's smokestack landscape
looks like a pagoda
in a Buddhist Temple.

In this woolen gray sky,
what pulls over my head
makes me warm sometimes.

After graduating college,
I split my nails.
Bag groceries.
Punch cash registers.

What right do I have
to discuss Van Gogh?
Rouge my cheeks?
Carry the tray
of "smart" conversation?

Leave the tray to the waitress, honey.
Poor broads don't scoop out knowledge
with the mashed potatoes and gravy.
Us guys count on food for the gut.

There's no geishas in Scranton.
Cut out the fantasy
of silk kimonos
and speaking Japanese.
Peel off those tight jeans.
Pop open a beer.

Because, And, If, But, Maybe, When, Maybe, As If: Why These Words Are Not All Conjunctions

I want a date
or at least a kiss
of the sly conversation
about 80s alternative rock
the Smiths and the Cure.

All I seize is a bite
from my overdone hot dog
and talk about whether or not
I like ketchup or mustard or relish
on my burned beef frank.

This is all I can expect
on a first date
as if pouring condiments
salvages the last seconds
of a waning weekend.

In France, Depeche Mode
is the new fashion.
On this deck,
an English rock band
who never made it
past synthesizers.

Those invented instruments
where one push of the key
creates an orchestra
false piano keys devour sound
a lion wiping drool
from his almost full lips.

Our blind date: an orchestra full of synthesizers.

Not even the 80s
the decade of bad hair
saves us.
I always thought the more hair spray
I could manager to wear
the lovelier I could be.

The proportion of proposals
for dates
to the semi-formal
to the homecoming
relied on the scientific formula
the high school basketball cheerleaders used.
Spray the shit out of the bangs.
Use as much *Aqua Net* as possible.

Their theory of action and reaction
didn't work for me.
I forgot to curl
the part in front.
I didn't use gel or mousse
before the hair spray.

On this blinder date: the equation wins.

A few drinks later,
All conjunctions and theories proved true
for an hour or two
the perfect hot dog
the perfect hair do
the perfect prom gown
I zip up or down.

You study
every branch
of biology, physiology, anatomy.
You acquire vast knowledge
about various body parts.

There is more than gravitational pull involved.

The most obscure trigonometric function
helped Picasso create Cubism
Kennedy's assassination
has something to do with mathematics
the solution flying
from the magic bullet
with the pull of a trigger.

On the blindest date
the aorta exploding
is not equal
to the conjunction of beer imploding
with your liver and mine
again and again.

I'll never understand
the power of trajectory.

Because as if and but maybe.

Letter's suffering
for the sake
of making us whole.

No Mr. Coffee For Mr. Sinatra

Frank's handling out glass martini answers.
I am asking what you might pick.
A teenage crush hasn't hit me in awhile.
I'm not near the age of ingénue.

My hair's too short
and my curves
voluptuous as some suitors brag
are not hips
you desire
to take home
and keep
like the coffee maker
with a timer beeping
as the beans are done.

When percolating the blend of lust,
my shape is considered reliable
as a machine that wakes you up
without the complication
time puts on us.

One night changes the conclusion
in ol' Mr. Coffee,
yes, another mister exists.
And he has hands.
As he uses his fingers.
And he talks long with his tongue.
He doesn't speak
with the angry groan
of an alarm.
I can't imagine shutting him off.

I dig Sinatra's soliloquy
not a Shakespearean sonnet.
Only the measured feeling10
about the guts of New Jersey.

Oh, Sinatra
Shakespeare had comedy and tragedy
Men playing women.
Frankie you had balls
when said balls
vibrate through a lounge singer's body
to the microphone
a jukebox flashes magic
for a girl who expected
to be as unrequited as Ophelia
remembering rosemary
instead of expecting touch.

32nd Sunday in Ordinary Time

In Kirby Park
we toss the frisbee
and witty repartee
because we read the Times everyday.
I see you.
I can't run through leaves
without shoes on.
There is a chance of stepping
into the expression on his face
as the sun slices
the separation of earth to sky.

At Halloween,
a blonde wig made me Marilyn
and thick bifocals framed you
into Arthur Miller.
Monroe's white dress rises.
Miller likes the intellect of panties
and all the dumbed down lace.

Two days later,
after the costumes are returned,
we chase this orange routine of plastic
one fluorescent orbit
after another.

Anointing For The Lonely Is Not A Sacrament

When I looked out the hospital window
where I was born
I saw St. Ann's steeples
thought why I was damn stupid
to not take a vocation seriously
but not those Immaculate Hearts
that taught me in school.

I wanted to be a Passionist sister.
The ones who carried
the suffering of Jesus
and his desire, too,
under the habit
under the smocks
in the body breathing
no matter what habits I wear.

With the days getting shorter,
I think it would be nice
to be buried
at St. Ann's.

The church where
Grandma took my Aunt Verna
Because she took care
where dentures and mind don't fit.
Verna pined over a boyfriend
from seventy years before.
Sacrifice can't be measured
like the temperature
on July novena days.

The church where my mom took us
with a stone grotto full
of seven day candles
to lay our hands on the porcelain St. Ann's
The statue –
a mom giving her young daughter advice
before she wasn't too old to mouth back.
Ann told Mary about being a decent kid
and all the usual parent things:
Don't stay out after dark.
Look out when you walk home from school.

Good St. Ann had no idea;
She'd be Christ's Grandmother.
Mary was the without original sin gal.
She didn't have to be reminded about being bad
or getting knocked up before marriage.
Her pregnancy was the Holy Spirit's job
after all.
She touched with fingers and hands
more intent on mothering
than all our disappointments of pleasure.

I looked out a window in the hospital.
My middle finger praised
with some attempt of adoration.
I lived, pale, titless, plugged with IVs
bald and in isolation.
I guess, almost monastic,
too much quiet and not enough belief.

When you've grown up with church steeples.
there's no one
to help you
wear death
like a wedding dress
no one to walk you down the isle.
to the end.

Smalltown Girls Don't Get Jesus, The Guy, Or A Decent Bouquet

It's the same old story.
The girl who hurts will
continue to do so.

She will be St. Gemma
who dresses in mourning clothes
because no saints
are ever supposed to show off
her pink lacy Victoria's Secret underwear
in Church.

This is the statue,
Babushka wearing ladies
wallow at her feet.
Give her the last roses
in the supermarket cooler.

The thought of giving life
is beautiful.
She might allow herself
a chance to cry.

She's a strong Italian sculpture.
She must redden her cheeks
in private.
When the flowers are so sweet and fresh,
chipped paint is now allowed.

Most get tired of
the perpetual night
of that lower chapel,
a cave
with few people,

without kindness of relatives
to remind her she must eat more
and make her bed before sleep.

She is a painted and molded vocation.
Worshippers leave rosaries and intentions
to ask for their daughter to get married
their son to find a new job.
She listens because she likes flowers.

She's just one miracle short
of receiving spring in her hands.

Book III
Transplanted Poems

(Unreleased Poems and Familiar Classics)

Table of Contents

Book III
Transplanted Poem

There's No Place Like Home

I sip lukewarm coffee
and find luxury
from an electric blue sky
and oaks leaning into the sun.

Living in this big house,
there's no one to talk to.
no fancy metaphors
to connect Christmas
to January's indifference.

I've been reading
your blogs
and the ache
in my hip has never been stronger.

How simple I am now.
I take care
of the stray sparrow or two
by the window
and see how your wife
refers to you as husband,

Here, the closet has clothes
dropped from its hangers.
The sweat pants and shirts

just don't know what to do
lounging on the floor
without a place
to find rest.

I am married to junk.
My couch is the only one
who touches me back.
stuffed cushions and all.

I limp in a kitchen
where I am a boarder
stealing Holiday chocolate fudge
while no one is around.

I am a widow
without a man
mourning a partner
I will never have
sitting across the table
drinking his orange juice
reaching out his hand.

Shatter

I sit in this big house
ready for company
as if I am poised
to run a marathon
to exhume the strength
in my legs.

I can believe
in this February thaw
that makes my porch
an extra room.

When I make love,
I picture you
except you're not
on the same mattress.

I know the truth is:
My limbs are weak.
The weather will turn cold.
My bed is not occupied
by another.

I listen to classical music
It's more honest than us.
Each instrument
a voice
I have to hear.

Single

I lay in bed.
I like the clean blankets.
My body is Rubensque
which means I can't be pretty
unless I lose 20 or so pounds.

I have an old fashioned nightshirt
that is blue green
I pretend it's a gown
and I am going to be royalty
at a ball.

The only soiree
I attend
is one
where comforter meets skin
to keep warm.

I have lace curtains
which don't block
the weather out.
But, they look nice.
Isn't that what
everyone desires anyway?
Making sure my hair is combed
and my closet
is still in shambles.

I lay (or is it more proper to say lie?)
The sheets are fingers
that kiss me back.

I stare at the green walls.

I could turn their color
into an ocean
where I sprawl on a beach chair.
Sip a margarita.
Watch the lifeguards get tanned.

Instead,
I just roll around.
Toss the blankets
as if all my worries
are caught under the bone
into places that only know
how to hurt.

Spring Cleaning

My hair doesn't want to lay right.
There's nothing I can do to control it.
The strands dance all over the place.
I try to find the right comb.

How could I blame them?
I haven't put anything in order
even my dishes go undone
don't even notice the pile
until the stack looks like a skyscraper.

I force myself to write everyday
as if these sentences
may scratch my signature
with some kind of grace.

The only thing I can't organize is you.
You're on my do list for a while now.
I neglect the facts
I use a wheelchair
and you are sexually attracted
to someone else.

So, come on.
Fill my days with mundane chores.
I'll spray down the bathroom with joy.
Scour the sink and smile.

First Date

She can't explain
how it will go
for her first date
after the transplant.

She buys herself
a new pair of pants
and a slinky little pink top
so that her boobs
can be noticed a little.

He wears khakis
and a crisp white shirt.
He slicks his hair back.

In the bathroom mirror,
he practices
the proper motion
of a kiss.

They will go
to a performance
about Billie Holiday.
A woman who
became close
not with the glance of a man
but by the fire of song.

She hopes
He will bring flowers.

She won't fault him
if he forgets
or doesn't buy
the right colored petals.

She scratches on lipstick
lke a kid crossing out
The wrong letter in a spelling test.
She makes her mouth
A burlesque dancer's red.

He nudges his tie
He fixes it
toward the middle of his chest
so she doesn't see
the button that doesn't behave
holding on by a string.

He locks the house.
He turns on the car.
and considers the choice
of radio station.
He chooses folk
with a guitar so sweet
it needs to be made
into a chocolate bar.

They meet at her house.
He holds a bouquet of daisies.
She puts them in a vase.
He sits at the kitchen table.
They reach out their hands.
As their fingers move
toward the sugar bowl,
they try to touch.

Solitary Confinement

I pull a hair from a mole on my chin.
I push up my bra straps.
I can't look
at the computer.

I complete the task
of throwing away
a used tea bag.
I eat at a table with
four tablecloths and one person
I do what I can
in a house big enough
for six people.
.
What does solitude
have to do with a mole on my chin?
Both are tired of being around
and would love to move away.

I need to build a fortress
around my imperfections.
Strong and tall.
One that can withstand:
The disco of snow.
The strip tease of daffodils.

I want to be as constant
as an icicle in December
as fleeting as a crocus in April.
These miracles get noticed.
However, small.

I Travel Miles For Cheap Stuff

I make the attempt to be clandestine.
not easy
when you are driving around
in a scooter in Walmart.
figuring out how to manuever the car
between the hundreds of lime colored bras
and the too small T shirts in the women's department.

The uniform for this place is red and blue flannels
I plop half and half and aluminum foil into the carriage.
This is a challenge to fight your way
past an old lady searching for the right Easter Basket
for her grandchildren.
The auburn bun almost ready
to fall out of her hair.

I'm the girl with no sense of North or South
and a bum leg.
I see semi bald men with bifocals
driving around
In their own Walmart car.
I get sad
because they are without company.

I chow down on a bacon lettuce tomato
in the Subway
at the back of the store
watching husband and wives
choose the exact type of orange juice
acting as if this selection
will get them some later on.

I wander
a nomad of good buys
steer toward the checkout
not sure
if my purchases
can fill my pantry up.

Mannequin Is Dutch For Man

I needed to go to Smith's Department Store to get to the Halloween Store in the mall.

Near the perfume counter, I saw a James Dean mannequin. He advertised the latest cologne for men: Rebellion. Mr. Dean was tough and gentle. Gentle and tough.

He liked fast cars and faster Hollywood chicks. He wore a red jacket and a look of intensity that would have me in five seconds. When I looked at the other department store mannequins, the only thing defining the difference between sexes is the chest. The well-defined male biceps and abs of James Dean before his crash.

Now, there was an idea. I needed a wig, a red coat, some tight blue jeans, a stuffing sock, and some cool boots. I could be James Dean. My old boyfriend said James Dean would make the perfect man for me. Dean never said a lot. It's probably why Jake and I broke up. He didn't like how I stared at the brunette models in fashion magazines.

I didn't care about the makeup and the clothes. I wanted to find all the curves she abandoned on the runway.

"Would you like a sample for your boyfriend?" The saleswoman shouted across the aisle. James Dean captivated me with the confidence of his solitude in the 1950's.

The 50's, where mothers wore pearls, an apron and popped pills instead of crying. No real men cried then either. Men only fixed things; like the car and the clogged drain.

The water in their tear ducts was plugged up and beyond repair.

The saleswoman didn't carry the size 2 fake nail profile of a perfume seller. She wore short brown locks with gray streaks right down the front. She squeezed into a pleated Jackie Kennedy pink pillbox suit. As I got closer, I say her stockings had a runner packed up with polish. She looked tired, but happy. She had this acceptance, not being anywhere but selling fragrances.

"Come over here honey. They put the display by oxford cloth shirts. God only knows why."

I walked to the counter and hesitated because I didn't have a man right now. It's funny, what I'll do for conversation. I'll go up to a stranger and talk about cologne for my invisible significant other.

"You're a lovely girl. You gotta have a guy. You're at the right age for kids.

That's great stuff. Kids, I mean. I wouldn't work, but I need the money. A little extra dough while they are in school."

I looked at her name tag. Sally. Yes, she definitely spoke Sally. She had this genuine mother quality. She's Sally, the mother of 2 kids, department store beauty guru.

She wore fuchsia reading glasses at the bottom of her nose. She lived with the vision of dollar store spectacles.

"Want to try a sample of Rebellion?"

"I'll try it. He always likes new colognes. Jake drenched himself in scent. He couldn't stop spraying.

"I think this is nice myself. My husband Bob really isn't into this stuff." He's a mechanic. I do bring it home for him anyway. Dirty hands six times a week. I throw away the Yuengling bottles he leaves by the couch. It's good to know I have someone around.

When the infomercial for Touch-N-Go love potion played some late Saturday

night, did Sally cuddle toward Bob as he dozed toward sleep?

"Mine's more high maintenance. Dry cleaned shirts. 40 dollar haircut.

Even a manicure. I tell him it's kind of weird to date a guy who takes better care of his nails than I do. He does give me trouble about not finishing school. Well, someday I will. We are going to a Halloween party and this will make me sexier.

I usually don't say this much.

She opened the case and showed me her sample bottle. It looked like a beer bottle with silver spray.

"All the girls will be on him like a fly on shit. Oh, excuse me. I apologize for the bad language. You'll have to keep an eye on him at the party. I'll bet you could be James Dean and Natalie Wood.

"Or maybe Elizabeth Taylor and Richard Burton." I said. Didn't they hate each other?"

"Not all the time."

Sally stopped talking for a minute. She adjusted the strap on her faux leather watch. She ached for a way to wind back what I had just said. She pretended not to hear me and continued on with her sales pitch.

"They usually don't do this. Give such a big sample out for free. She handed me Rebellion. I held the container like a mother holds a baby for the first time. In the transfer from her hand to mine, her nurturing collapsed in my palm.

For a moment, I longed to kiss her lips. In this movie, she would kiss back. James Dean and the manager with paisley tie would stand and look. They'd be the audience for a 30 something loner and a middle age woman making out under all that fluorescence.

With my ex, I closed my eyes. During this film, my eyes stayed open. They didn't have to fight to look close.

I leaned against the counter; infatuated with the brunette counter Mom. I must be a creep. I must be lonesome. This scene was perfect with James Dean as our voyeur. He was the salesman for unattached Halloweeners and perfume selling moms who can't figure out attraction has no answers.

"Lemme get you a bag. I hope he likes this. Come back and buy some." "He will."

"We might get a James Dean look-alike to promote the cologne."

"I didn't know they even had James Dean look-alikes. They do have Elvis…"

"The mannequin is doing wonders for sales. He was quite the sex symbol in his time. What's your man's name? Ya keep calling him he."

"Jake."

I clutched the bottle. She brushed my hand again with her press-on fingertips. She grabbed Windex and started to wipe down the collar. Sally left streaks.

"Get James Dean here soon."

"He's comin'. Tell Jake to come in here and buy some more."

"I will."

"Never mind James Dean when ya gotta good man. No use lookin' at the merchandise when you've already got something wonderful. I sure know that."

Sally straightened her jacket; tugged at her ring, twisted her band around and let the gold slip between her finger. She hesitated before she picked the ring up. She stared off and didn't say goodbye.

I walked out of Smith's and sprayed on some Rebellion. The scent of a man almost belongs on my skin.

Insecure Thy Name Is Jennifer Ann

When they wrote the word insecure
the they
Those Oxford English scholars
had me in their high intelligence quotients
for all eternity.

Even though I was not conceived
those men who worshipped Shakespeare
thought
let's put a picture
of a girl
who looks like a Jennifer Ann
near the word
and my neurotic nature
was drawn
before sperm met egg
and bore me into 1973.

I couldn't escape
The Grandeur of these Grammar Gods.
those men who wore graduation hats
as a matter of fashion.
They adorned me
with the name: Shy.

In preschool,
I was doomed
to the title:
Jennifer Noodles.
Be picked last for dodge ball
be a failure
at a handstand in gym

I learned to hate pep rallies.
because I was too fat
to fit into
those green and white cheerleader skirts.

Yes,
This sounds pathetic.
I admit.

In college,
I became the poet type.
I mumbled a lot
(and maybe still do)
cursed my lot
in black clothes
and bad writing
with too much alliteration.

Maybe those Oxford anal retentive masters
of the meaning of things
could rescind this curse
so I could cease
from moving from insecure to neurotic
and back again.
My anxiety
an earthquake shifting
the heart's tectonic plate.

Damn you,
fools of etymology
and cutting
a Catholic school girl
with badly permed hair
into pieces.

Take back my figure drawing
from the dictionary.
Release me
from the spell
of being awkward.
trying to push glasses up
even though
I have contacts.
The dreaded expectation
of the next zit
on my face
Solitude waiting to burst open
and bloom.

The Single Gal's Polka

During your wedding,
I caught the bouquet .
I look at this as serious.
I get the garter and all.
I take all this as a studious effort.
One false move
and even the roses
will lose their virginity.

My Sir Anonymous stands there
with a bouquet of daisies
and shiny wingtips
ready to ask that inevitable question
I crumble under the answer no.

Someday, I think there will be
another smiling Polish man
with a ruffled tuxedo suit
that I could mutter yes too
being so almost sure--
I'd accept the engagement

Then, I would dance the Polka.
Not just any polka,
Jan Lewan,
who courts all those ladies
who get married
with romantic Polka beats
as if the words romantic and Polka
can be used in the same sentence
without laughing or falling asleep.

Tara, sister,
I want to be as sure as you are
putting your arms
around an Eastern European gentleman
being so confident in how
to make ghumpkis and pierogis
that the recipe is not needed.

I run before
I have to boil water for tea.

When the reception's almost over,
I sit out the last dance.
Watch my flowers start to wilt
one carnation at a time.

I Admire Helen Dzik

The name of our team
said it all
The Maids
Maybe that's why
the softball committee
put a dress factory worker
and single broad
as coach.

She was the Polish stock
who didn't comb her hair
wore polyester pants
smoked
and probably drank
good potato vodka
when we'd lose again.

No one called her
an old maid, or old.
She played tough.
When she stood
on the first base line
and said to run,
you better damn well run.

This field was her joy.
This brief respite
from sewing hems
because where
a softball flies
is not as predictable
as finding the perfect stitch.

I didn't understand
the game
make her smoke less,
sorrow more.
No one on the bleachers
to wave to her or smile.

When the shortstop
couldn't catch
that oh so easy line drive,
Helen screamed.

We gave the other team
so many chances to score.
The spectator might have thought
we were the farthest thing
besides maids.

I caught that ball
in the outfield
all that hard solitude
in my glove

before I even knew
what made Helen hurt
was outside the fence
as I threw toward home.

Professional Resume For Poets Who Don't Fit The Job Description

*Dear Writers, please submit only the most tailored language in
our literary journal.
Loose fitting literature need not apply.*

Emily had to wear a corset
but most poems lace so tight
No reader knows;
there's a Dickinson underneath.

Academics button and zipper up books
so much
they forget mortal sin exists.
If they'd allow the writer
time to undress,
critics everywhere would die mortified.

Their overeducated hearts will learn
all alphabets breath more
when one gives
the serious countenance
a chance to squirm beyond intellect
into the spelling of forgiving skin.

Herr PHD Professors,
Allow letters to touch
fingertips and tongues.
Strip off
The brown-corduroy-jacket-with-the-patches lyric.

At the Harvest Ball,
good daily verse
sits in the gymnasium bleachers.
Nerdy four-eyed words with moon crater zits
wait for that special someone
who doesn't need
the perfect line break to dance.

Exultation Over Fried Chicken

I joy in the exoskeleton of chicken.
a thick shell made of grease and heat.
We bite that shell off
and eat.

There is a happiness
that vegetable oil and meat
fills between our teeth.
The miracle of this kitchen table
is a delicious and holy feast.

This meal gives me
one leg or thigh
more of satisfaction,
I treasure eating dinner
with no paper plate underneath.
Dinner wakes our grief
as crumbs of our beloved fall.

When you're done with supper,
you kiss me.
Oh, all the lips can do
eat, talk and offer comfort
to the living
who can't forget
the dead at our feet.

Peonies In Smalltown Backyards

You take me outside to the garden.
Eden across
from the General Hospital.
This Wednesday
takes on the myth of Adam and Eve
We pick peonies in a smalltown backyard
just ripe, just what is needed
to make me believe
this may be right.

Peonies, pink flowers in a vase,
dying stems that suck up water
and still want more.
Luscious bursts of color
the sweet wild
I will never hold.
I want to believe in peonies
as petals fall before summer begins.

Pas De Deux

Twirl, spin
until you go
from 4 to 31
at McCann's School of Dance
to the point
where you stand
toes turned five digits
counting to perfect

5,4,3,2,1...

This from a girl
who lasted one class
whose closest trip to Julliard
is watch the 8 o clock public TV version
of Swan Lake
by the New York City Ballet.

I think it was the fascination
with those ever so black leotards
scraping my skin
choreographing my skeleton
to dance
Into and not away from flesh

How foolish
not to learn
how to arabesque
standing at the tow bar
growing taller.

I only stayed
in Ms. MeCann's ballet

for one hour.
Maybe it was because
I couldn't pull my hair
into a bun
like the other kindergarten prima donnas.
That trauma
of having my long hair
severed my scissors.

My preschool teacher
said my curls
caught the wind
the wrong way.

If you ask me
about modern ballet
I'll throw you some names
Martha Graham
Alvin Ailey.

Make myself appear
as cultured as the pearls
who only throw a glare
inside the jewelry box
and forget the glow
around my neck.

I want to twirl for you
but I don't know
the meaning
never mind the step
French doesn't plie along these lips
and our mouths
don't grace the tongue's pirhouette.
Two muscles bend

to meet the other's motion.

You don't surrender
as a principal ballet dancer should
lifting me toward sky
requires too much precision
and our lips don't drift
beyond this Slovak kitchen.

Your house, a replica of my grandmother's,
gravy stains the stove
and tired tablecloth
sleeps under the weight
of spoiled sour cream.
Butter erupts yellow volcanos
from its pink glass house.

Your Mom and Dad
waltz through air
While Duke Ellington plays,
your parents are voyeurs
as you reach to kiss me
in the space in the kitchen
near the back door.

But this house
will never be a place for culture
or love of culture
even Degas
glorified prostitutes
as ballerinas.
Hookers posing as dancers
because this paid
the same as sex.

The prostitute always find the right position
on canvass
suspended in air
stretching toward flight.

I leap somewhere
between her azure blue
and your gray muscle
down below
pulsing toward our Pas De Deux
struggling to fumble
on pointe.

Room 321, ICU

My poetry mom
is the procreator of my letters
and birthed me alive
long after
sperm made egg
and said yes.

Under Japanese maples,
We swallowed box wine and phrases like
"You can publish my poems after"
and
"I'll be Scranton's Emily Dickinson",
You laugh.

You used to smoke Virginia Slims.
but, now, the ventricles
can even pump knowledge.
The aorta is a muscle, after all.
It gets tired sometimes.

There is no margin for error
when blood is involved.
I try not to use was,
as if
inviting was
welcomes the passive voice.

Forgive me that
I can't let the ventilator,
beat breath.
I can't let
this violence speak for you.

I follow your advice,
Good writers avoid sentiment
and embrace space.
This time, though,
I break the rule.
I don't want to leave so much room.

Elephants Don't Forget

The smallest things. The size of a peanut. Their age. Your heart hollows against the bare Sunday afternoon. You rock in your chair, reckless. A 20 year-old woman in an 84 year old body, rips you into and out of stories.

With your stockings rolled down, you bear your legs and the stubble of ten thousand days. The hairs grow frail and wispy as if the 1940's somehow revived you on a February day. Your brown hair singes the air, waving in salute to WWII and the railroads.

Snow and ice carve honesty. You tell me about your sister, Veronica, as if you just baked bread. You, ice skated at Nay Aug's Lincoln Lake with a 19 inch waist, ironed and starched clothes, could not press perfect into your mother's eyes.

All the men adored Veronica. Her breasts lifted beyond South Sixth Avenue. D cup size always promotes more travel, trips to New York City on the Delaware and Lackawanna. Your cup size, B to be precise, only allowed for short trips to Washington where you worked and sent back money. You would give your cup size, shoe size, dress size. No size fit.

When you didn't sew into homemade clothes, you tried to make clothes for a husband. The backyard wedding complete with chickens and Polish and Ukrainian families fight. Cocks of the human and animal variety. Maybe it was the language barrier.

A few fights later, the violin dripped polkas. The night air stirred with the sweet of paska bread just coming out of the oven. The raisins and fluffy dough rose with the violinist's song. And you hang on to the melody.

Four children later. These pink brocade curtains are wrinkled. This house cost five thousand dollars 40 years ago. Rocking chairs weep in years. You wanted no more salty soup out of a can. Your silver hair rolls into curlers.

You are half dosing now. Sunday skates into the night ice of Monday. The simple slip that you don't know is coming, but are prepared for. You try to salt all the walks. You wait for the fall to happen. Then, hope the bread may not be bad.

On TV, 60 Minutes. This show sifts through age. You are 84 again. African elephants are creating art that costs five thousand dollars or more. They are the Jackson Pollacks of the jungle. They can structure the canvass with the splashed strokes of a brush. What memory and art can do. You can't believe how they paint, even if the long trunk gets in the way.

In the morning, your rocking chair remembers you. The jaw drops as if to say. You are not the elephants. You are a mammal. Not able to speak, but you will never forget.

Made in the USA
Middletown, DE
05 February 2020

84172333R00139